# Mosquitoes

by Cheryl Coughlan

Consulting Editor: Gail Saunders-Smith, Ph.D.

Consultant: Gary A. Dunn, Director of Education,
Young Entomologists' Society

## Pebble Books

an imprint of Capstone Press
Mankato, Minnesota

Pebble Books are published by Capstone Press
1710 Roe Crest Drive, North Mankato, Minnesota 56003
www.capstonepress.com

Printed in the United States of America in North Mankato, Minnesota.
102015   009281R

*Library of Congress Cataloging-in-Publication Data*
Coughlan, Cheryl.
    Mosquitoes/by Cheryl Coughlan.
    p. cm.—(Insects)
    Includes bibliographical references (p. 23) and index.
    Summary: Simple text and photographs describe the physical
characteristics of mosquitoes.
    ISBN-13: 978-0-7368-0243-7 (hardcover)
    ISBN-10: 0-7368-0243-6 (hardcover)
    ISBN-13: 978-0-7368-8214-9 (softcover pbk.)
    ISBN-10: 0-7368-8214-6 (softcover pbk.)
    1. Mosquitoes—Juvenile literature. [1. Mosquitoes.] I. Title. II. Series: Insects
(Mankato, Minn.)
QL536.C788      1999
595.77'2—dc21
                                          98-43745
                                              CIP
                                              AC

## Note to Parents and Teachers

The Insects series supports national science standards for units on the
diversity and unity of life. The series shows that animals have features that
help them live in different environments. This book describes and
illustrates the parts and lives of mosquitoes. The photographs support early
readers in understanding the text. The repetition of words and phrases
helps early readers learn new words. This book also introduces early
readers to subject-specific vocabulary words, which are defined in the
Words to Know section. Early readers may need assistance to read some
words and to use the Table of Contents, Words to Know, Read More,
Internet Sites, and Index/Word List sections of the book.

# Table of Contents

Mosquitoes are insects.

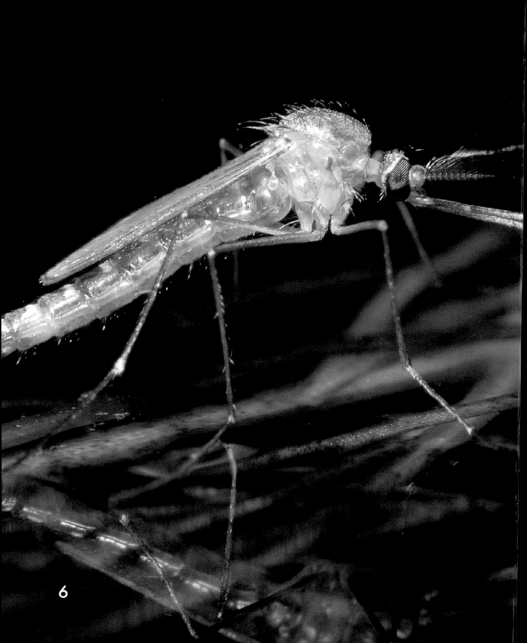

6

Mosquitoes live
near water.

8

Mosquitoes buzz.

10

Mosquitoes have
a thin body.

wings

Mosquitoes have
two wings.

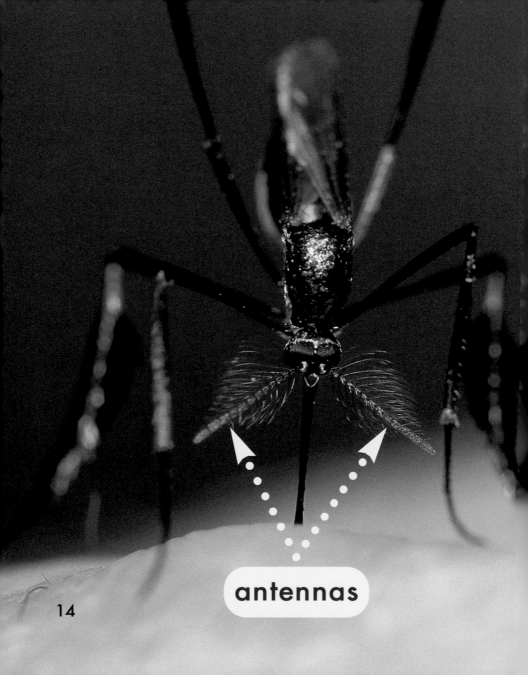

antennas

Mosquitoes have
two hairy antennas.

proboscis

Mosquitoes have
a proboscis.

Mosquitoes drink
plant juices.

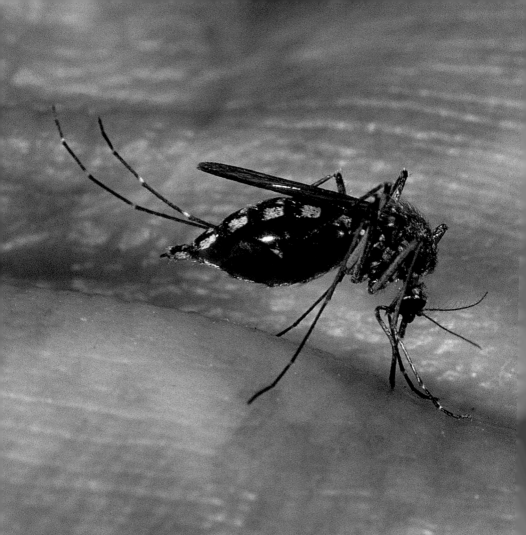

20

Female mosquitoes
suck blood from
people and animals.

# Words to Know

**antenna**—a feeler on an insect's head; mosquitoes have two hairy antennas that can sense movement.

**blood**—the fluid that moves through the bodies of people and animals; only female mosquitoes suck blood from people and animals.

**female**—an animal that can give birth to young animals or lay eggs; female mosquitoes suck blood from people and animals so their eggs can grow.

**insect**—a small animal with a hard outer shell, three body parts, six legs, and two antennas; insects may have two or four wings; mosquitoes have two wings and are a type of fly.

**proboscis**—a long, tube-shaped mouthpart; mosquitoes use their proboscis to drink plant juices and to suck blood.

**wing**—a movable part of an insect that helps it fly; mosquitoes beat their wings about 1,000 times each second.

# Read More

**Hunt, Joni Phelps.** *Insects.* Closeup. Parsippany, N.J.: Silver Burdett Press, 1995.

**Ryden, Hope.** *ABC of Crawlers and Flyers.* New York: Clarion Books, 1996.

**Snedden, Robert.** *What Is an Insect?* San Francisco: Sierra Club Books for Children, 1993.

# Internet Sites

FactHound offers a safe, fun way to find Internet sites related to this book.

Go to *www.facthound.com*

He'll fetch the best sites for you!

# Index/Word List

**Word Count: 39**
**Early-Intervention Level: 7**

**Editorial Credits**

Damian C. Koshnick, editor; Timothy Halldin, cover designer; Kimberly Danger, photo researcher

**Photo Credits**

Bill Johnson, 10, 12, 18, 20
David M. Dennis/Tom Stack and Associates, 14
Dwight R. Kuhn, cover, 4, 6, 8, 16
GeoIMAGERY/Joe Warfel, 1